15-42

behavior disorders:

helping children with behavioral problems

by

a. lee parks
university of idaho

thomas n. fairchild
series editor
danial b. fairchild
illustrator

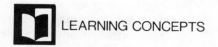 LEARNING CONCEPTS

Second Printing, 1977

Library of Congress Cataloging in Publication Data

Parks, A   Lee.
  Behavior disorders.

  (Mainstreaming series)
  1. Problem children—Education.   I.   Title.
LC4801.P35   371.9'3   76-50651
ISBN 0-89384-007-6

Learning Concepts
2501 N. Lamar
Austin, Tx. 78705

dedication

To Judy, Rick, and Shawn

acknowledgments

I would like to express my sincere appreciation to a number of people who have helped in the preparation of this manuscript.

For their assistance in reviewing the manuscript:

Tom Fairchild, Editor of the MAINSTREAMING SERIES, who assisted in bringing order out of chaos.

Marvin Fine, my superb mentor at the University of Kansas.

Henry Leland, colleague at The Ohio State University, who has an incredible record for being right.

Dale Schmaljohn and Ken Dunbar, school psychologists in the Boise Public Schools, Idaho.

Len Ellis, employed by the Idaho Division of Special Education.

Jean Fitzgerald, Supervisor, Child Evaluation Clinic, Cedar Rapids, Iowa.

For their assistance in brainstorming cartoon ideas, I would like to thank Judy Parks and Carolyn Fairchild.

For typing the final manuscript, I would like to express appreciation to Shellie West.

foreword

In the past, the educational needs of exceptional children were met by removing them from the "mainstream" of the regular classrooms, and serving them in a variety of segregated self-contained special classes. The trend in the '70's is educating exceptional children in the least restrictive educational setting; that is, as close as possible to their normal peers. This concept of "mainstreaming" exceptional children has received considerable support from within and outside the educational community. Although self-contained special classes will always be a meaningful alternative for some children, the personal and educational needs of many exceptional children can better be served in the regular class program with the supportive services of ancillary personnel and/or resource room help.

With the emphasis on "mainstreaming," the regular classroom teacher is now expected to meet the needs of exceptional children in his or her classroom along with all the other children in the class. The problem is that most regular classroom teachers have little or no preparation in the area of educating exceptional children. Regular classroom teachers need basic information regarding the various exceptionalities, and more specifically, practical suggestions which they can employ to enhance the "mainstreamed" exceptional child's personal and educational development.

The MAINSTREAMING SERIES was written to fill this need. Each book in the SERIES addresses itself to one area of exceptionality allowing teachers to select from the SERIES according to their interest or need. Each text provides information designed to correct misconceptions and stereotypes, and to improve the teacher's understanding of the exceptional child's uniqueness. Numerous practical suggestions are offered which will help the teacher work more effectively with the exceptional child in the "mainstream" of the regular classroom.

Currently, there is a great deal of controversy surrounding the use of categories and labels. The books in the SERIES are organized according to categories of exceptionality because the content within each book is only relevant for a child with a specific handicapping condition. The intent is not to propagate labeling; in fact, labeling children is inconsistent with the philosophy of the SERIES. The books address themselves to behaviors, and how teachers can work with these behaviors in exceptional children. The books in the SERIES are categorized— not the children. The books are categorized in order to cue teachers to the particular content for which they might be looking.

There is much truth in the old saying, "A picture is worth a thousand words." A cartoon format was used for each book in the MAINSTREAMING SERIES as a means of sustaining interest and emphasizing important concepts. The cartoon format also allows for easy, relaxed reading. We felt that teachers, being on the firing line all day, would be more likely to read and refer to our material, than to a lengthy text filled with theory and jargon. Typically cartoons exaggerate, stereotype, and focus on weaknesses. I sincerely hope that these cartoons do not offend any children, parents, or professionals, because that is not the purpose for which they were intended. They are intended to make you think.

I hope you find this book helpful in your work with mainstreamed exceptional children, or with any other children, since they are all special.

THOMAS N. FAIRCHILD
SERIES EDITOR

contents

3. how can i help?

introduction

Behavior disorders are common in our society. Teachers and parents are becoming increasingly concerned about these problems in children. Behavior disorders are referred to in a variety of ways depending on the severity of the problem and the theoretical approach of the diagnostician. Some of the terms used are neurosis, psychosis, obsessive-compulsive, autistic and character disorder. These are only a few of the terms that are used. A major point of this book is that labels are less useful than what can be done to help such children. Labels often have the effect of making diagnosis an end in itself, rather than directly leading to treatment. Even though this book presents some characteristics of behavior disordered children and theoretical approaches to why they exhibit these behaviors, the major emphasis (chapter 3) is on what teachers and parents can do to help children with behavioral problems. The bias of this book is clearly behavioral.

chapter 1

what are behavior disordered children like?

This chapter describes behavior disordered children. The following behaviors will be discussed:

Aggression

Fears

Shyness, Reclusiveness

Lying

Sadness, Crying

Self-stimulation, Destructiveness

These, however, are only a few of the behaviors found among behavior disordered children. The point is that most of these behaviors are not unique in themselves. What makes them a problem is their severity and/or chronicity.

In our society today we see a great variety of behaviors. What is normal and what is abnormal? Many teachers and parents are concerned about the behavior of their children. They may be concerned to the point that they have sought professional advice. This book was written to explain behavioral disorders, why they occur, and what parents and teachers can do to help these children.

What are behavior disordered children like? First, they fit
no single description. They are so different that one
definition is relatively valueless. The types of behaviors,
as well as their severity, are extremely variable from one
child to another.

Some behaviorally disordered children are very aggressive. They may be aggressive toward objects or . . .

. . . they may direct their aggressive behavior toward people. It may be physical . . .

. . . or verbal aggression.

This aggression may be extreme and overt in some children. In others it may be a very subdued, yet persistent as in the case of a child who regularly engages in secret mildly destructive acts.

Just because a particular child is aggressive in one setting does not mean he or she may behave that way in another. In fact, this statement can be generally made for most of the other behaviors that will be discussed. We have all seen the difference in children's behavior between school, home and social settings.

Some behavior disordered children could be described as very anxious. Often they don't appear to know why. They are just anxious. They are very unrelaxed and expect the worst; yet, they're not sure when this terrible thing will happen or what it will be.

Others know exactly what to be afraid of—trees, cats, dogs, snakes, cars, heights, water, small places, etc. . . . .

. . . and school! Fear of school is very common among young children, but less common at older ages.

This fear of school in children has been known to generalize to other settings like grocery stores, making it impossible for the child to go shopping. This is a severe and unusual example.

Some children are very shy or reclusive. They do not talk to others. Some spend much time away from others . . .

. . . by spending hours on end in their room or in other secluded places. As with earlier examples, this behavior may be minor or very severe.

A frequently observed behavior is lying. This varies from small fibs . . .

. . . to enormous whoppers

Sometimes the lies are used to cover up other misbehaviors.

Despite the best efforts of teachers and parents, it is often very difficult to stop some children from telling "untruths".

Sadness and crying are behaviors exhibited by some behavior disordered children. They cry for unapparent reasons and are sad for prolonged periods of time. There may have once been a good reason for this behavior, but now the reason is gone.

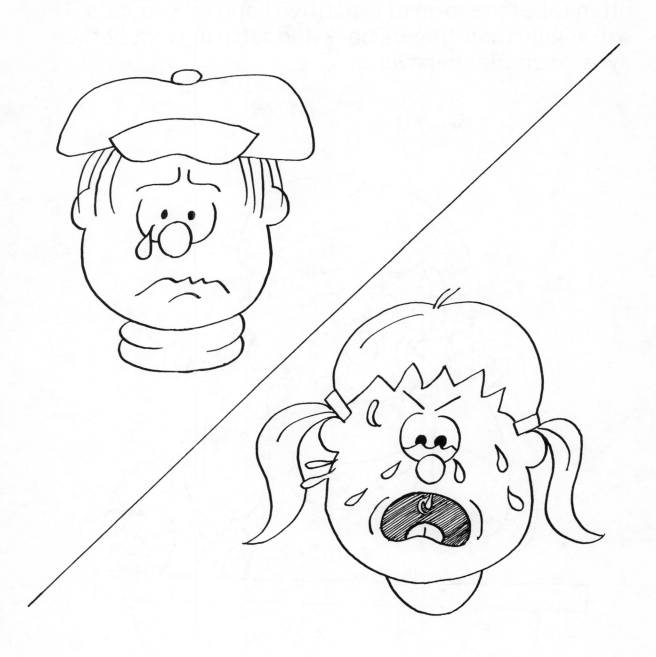

A few behavior disordered children have severe problems that are unfamiliar to most of us. Some children involve themselves in self-stimulation for hours upon hours. This often takes the form of repetitive hand movements. They will wiggle their fingers back and forth in front of their eyes, or similar behaviors.

These children are often extremely withdrawn, speaking little or not at all with others. They may sit and rock for hours. They may appear not to see or hear others in the room.

Some of these children are self-destructive. That is, they engage in self-hitting, scratching, or biting. Again, such children are very rare.

Obviously, there is no single description of a child with a behavior disorder. Behavior disordered children come in many forms, with greater and lesser degrees of severity.

They all do have one thing in common, however . . .

IMPORTANT NOTICE

The behaviors of behavior disordered children are
not that much different from the behaviors of
"normal" children. The difference is primarily
a matter of amount of behavior—not kind.
If a child exhibits too much or too
little of a behavior, it may be seen
as a behavior disorder. It may
also be seen as a problem if a
child exhibits the behavior
in the wrong setting.

For example, aggressiveness is not a problem. It is when the child becomes excessively aggressive that there is a problem. Too little aggression can also be a problem.

To have fears is also normal. In fact, it is often very useful to have fears.

It is only when they become excessive that there is a problem. If a fear interrupts other normal necessary functions, it can cause a real problem for the child.

This notion of behavior disorders being a matter of too much or too little behavior, is true even for self-stimulating, repetitive behaviors like rocking. A moderate amount of rocking is relaxing.

Rocking all day, however, can interfere with most normal self-care skills.

A final point to be made in this section is that different people have different standards for what constitutes "excessive" behavior. Some teachers are typically less tolerant of activity in the classroom than others. The same child in the same setting might be judged normal by one teacher and behavior disordered by another. But the term behavior disordered, as psychologists typically use it, refers to children with atypical behaviors as judged by most observers.

The same point applies to different settings. What is accepted as normal behavior at home or on the playground may not be accepted as normal for the classroom. This is a case of too much behavior in the wrong setting.

REVIEW

Remember . . .

—There is a great diversity of behaviors exhibited in our society.

—What constitutes a behavior disorder cannot be stated simply. There is no single definition.

—Examples of behavior disorders include aggression, fears, shyness/reclusiveness, lying, sadness/crying, and self-stimulation/destructiveness.

—A behavior in itself is not a problem. It can become a problem if it is exhibited too much or too little, or in the wrong setting.

—Different people (different cultures) have different standards regarding what constitutes a problem behavior.

—Different settings require different behaviors. What is acceptable behavior in one may not be acceptable behavior in another.

chapter 2

---

why do behavior disordered children behave the way they do?

People have sought answers to the problems of human behavior for years. There are many theories which seek to explain the causes of typical and unusual behavior. Most of these theories can be put into four groups. This section will present some information on the four major approaches and how they deal with behavior disordered children.

The four major approaches are:

Psychodynamic

Psychoneurological

Psychoeducational

Behavioral

This chapter presents the basic assumptions of each of the four approaches. It will shown how each:

- Explains "causes" of disordered behavior
- Diagnoses disordered behavior
- Treats disordered behavior

Some readers may feel that this chapter has at least two limitations. First, the discussion of the approaches are of the most cursory sort. Second, the cartoon caricatures present a stereotypic picture of each of the approaches. The author is aware that a person's favorite theory is "a thing of joy forever." Dogmatic adherence to theory serves little purpose. They become less important when data are the focal point for decision-making. Often, it is only the rhetoric that varies between theories, not the professional's actual behaviors toward the client. It is this concern for the pragmatic that has shaped this chapter more than the need to make complete statements about theoretical points of view.

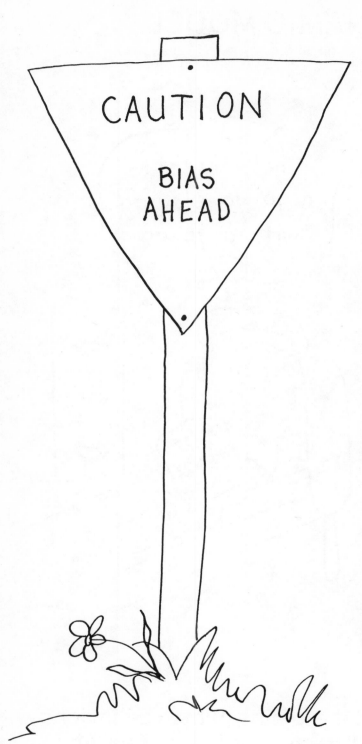

The reader is cautioned that there is a bias in this chapter. It clearly favors the behavioral approach to explaining behavior disorders. Consequently, chapter 3 "How Can I Help?" will be a more complete description of treatment procedures from the behavioral point of view. Treatments will be dealt with in this chapter only to the extent that they will make each theory's approach to the question "why?" clearer.

PSYCHODYNAMIC MODEL

The psychodynamic model explains human behavior by hypothesizing that "inner happenings" are the real causes of behavior.

"Inner happenings" refers to the id, ego, and superego, and how they interact to cause behavior. The id is a primitive urge. The superego is an inhibiting, very idealistic force. The ego arbitrates between these two forces to balance their various needs.

Intrapsychic conflicts can arise as a result of unresolved needs, imparied parent-child relations, and other factors. This approach looks to the past history of the child for causes of the disorder. A **single** past event may be seen as very important in causing current behavior.

To diagnose a problem the psychodyamic approach obtains case histories, conducts personal interviews, and administers projective tests. These tests are designed to enable the child to verbalize inner conflicts, even though the child may not be aware that that is what he or she is doing.

Treatment generally takes the form of counseling, play therapy, or psychoanalysis. The aim is to help the child understand the inner conflict leading to the problem behaviors. The observable behaviors are merely symptoms of an underlying problem.

PSYCHONEUROLOGICAL MODEL

The psychoneurological approach to behavior disorders is less encompassing than the psychodynamic model. It does not deal with all behavior disorders. Such factors as delayed maturation and inadequate neurological development are considered to be indirectly related to disorders in behavior. The psychoneurological approach explains some behavior disorders as being the result of injury to the brain. This injury causes emotional instability, hyperactivity, and impulsivity.

This injury to the brain is usually referred to as "Minimal Brain Dysfunction (MBD)". It is called minimal because it is so slight that it is generally undetectable. It is a diffuse condition because no one really knows where it is. A child may be diagnosed as having "MBD" if he behaves like people who do have identifiable brain damage.

To diagnose, the psychoneurological model relies on electroencephalograph (EEG) findings (brain wave patterns), neurological examinations, developmental histories, and current reports from parents and teachers. These findings suggest whether or not the child has the "MBD" syndrome.

How do we treat brain damage? We don't. It is the behavior that is treated. One of the most frequently used procedures is the use of stimulant drugs. These drugs often have the paradoxical effect of reducing the problem behavior if the child is below the age of adolescence.

Another procedure is education and training. The child is taught new ways to behave. Often the new skills are taught indirectly. That is, excessive activity might be handled indirectly by teaching coordination.

PSYCHOEDUCATIONAL MODEL

The psychoeducational approach, referred to by some as the diagnostic-remedial approach, deals primarily with the behavior disorder called "learning disabilities." Consequently, this model only seeks to explain learning behaviors, not other more general functioning. Learning disabilities are the result of "internal processing" difficulties which affect visual, auditory, or fine-motor functioning.

To diagnose behavior disorders (learning problems), the psychoeducational approach uses tests to detect where the internal processing difficulties exist. They also make direct observations and acquire case histories.

Remediation is prescribed to correct the "internal processing" problem. If successful this should improve the child's ability to learn.

Some professionals consider a learning disability a behavior disorder because it clearly is a behavioral deficit that both directly and indirectly causes problems for the child. Some readers may not be comfortable with the notion that a learning disability is a form of behavior disorder. If so, please cut this and the preceding two pages from the book.

BEHAVIORAL MODEL

The behavioral model explains behavior as being the result of environmental conditions—behaviors are learned. To the behaviorist, the present is much more important than the past. The primary question is "What in the environment is perpetuating the inappropriate behavior?" Environment includes those things with which the individual comes into contact. For the child, some of the more important environmental events include parents, teachers, peers, and school work.

The environment affects behavior in three ways. It maintains behavior at its present level, increases behavior or decreases it. The behaviorists state:

- Behaviors maintain or increase if they are reinforced (rewarded).

- Behaviors decrease if they are punished, or if they are not occasionally reinforced.

Though this sounds straight forward, many have found that the simplicity of these principles is deceptive.

According to behaviorists, children with behavior disorders learn their inappropriate behaviors like all other children learn their appropriate behaviors. Often, undesirable behaviors are inadvertently reinforced. A classic example is the "bad" boy in the room whom the teacher keeps in at recess. She is inadvertently encouraging what she is seeking to discourage.

In other cases behavior disorders are the result of lack of reinforcements for appropriate behavior or, in some cases, punishment. Lack of reinforcement deprives the child of the opportunity to learn.

Receiving only punishment teaches the child to behave in a punishing way toward others.

Diagnosis, per se, is not done by the behaviorist. Diagnosis implies assessment of a "deeper" cause. The behaviorist prefers to look for more observable causes— the environmental conditions under which the behavior was learned and maintained. He or she looks for the events that reinforce or maintain the current undesired behavior or punish the desired behavior. In addition, an objective measurement of the behavior is important. How frequently does Leon hit others? Or, how long does Loretta remain by herself? This provides a measure of how severe the problem is, as well as a running account of how the behavior is changing over a period of time.

Treatment is provided by directly teaching the desired behavior. The primary means of establishing a new behavior is to reinforce it whenever it or an approximation of it occurs.

Treatment is a matter of increasing desired behaviors and decreasing undesired ones using a step by step process. It is primarily a problem of learning, as opposed to resolution of inner dynamic conflicts or dealing with brain damage.

chapter 3

how can i help?

TEACHERS AND PARENTS
CAN HELP MOST.

This chapter discusses the ways teachers and parents can help the behavior disordered child. It presents procedures that can be used in school and home settings. These procedures are not difficult but they do require practice. All of them are based on the assumption that disorders in behavior are learned and that new more appropriate behaviors can also be learned.

This Chapter Will Present Information On:

- Applying consequences to behaviors
- Shaping behaviors
- Measurement and graphing
- Applied examples in school and home settings

APPLYING CONSEQUENCES TO BEHAVIORS

As stated earlier, reinforcements (pleasant consequences) can be used by teachers and parents to increase a child's behavior.

You must keep a couple of things in mind:

First, be consistent!

Often teachers and parents fail, not because they weren't using a good procedure, but because they weren't consistent. You often hear, "oh, I tried that once." Once is not enough. You must be consistent day after day for a reasonable number of days. If the behavior has been around a long time, it is going to take some time and energy to affect change.

Second, not everyone likes the same things!

Another error often made is assuming that everyone likes the same things you do. Just because you and "most everyone" like a certain food doesn't mean that "everyone" does. This is true for all types of reinforcers. Also, any single reinforcer tends to lose its reinforcing value after a period of time.

Here are a few ways to identify a reinforcer:

- Ask the child.

- Observe the child. What he or she does a lot of is generally what he or she likes.

- Use what has worked in other situations with that child or others.

- Give him or her a choice. (As stated earlier, tastes change from time to time.)

MENU

Reinforcers come in many forms. These include:

SOCIAL REINFORCERS	ACTIVITY REINFORCERS	TANGIBLE REINFORCERS

Praise from adults like:
  "Very good"
  "I like that"
  "Nice job"
  "Wow!"
  "Super!"
  "Far out!"
 	
Physical contact like:
  Pat on back
  Rub head
  Squeeze arm
  Kiss
  Gentle touch
  A "playful" pinch
	Listening to records and radio
	Watching TV
	Playing outside
	Playing with games
	Talking to others
	Sitting alone quietly
	Coloring
	Extra recess
		Stars
		Inexpensive toys
		Tokens
		Food

Reinforcers should be as **natural** as possible. That is, they should be typical to the setting in which they are being used. Money is typical to some settings, but not to the classroom. Praise and grades are typical to the classroom, but not to other settings like factory work. Sometimes it is necessary to use less natural reinforcers, at least for awhile. It may be the only way in which a new behavior can be established. But after awhile the parent or teacher should try to find a more natural reinforcer. Two advantages to these kinds of reinforcers are that they are more readily available and parents and teachers are more receptive to using them.

Punishment may also be used when dealing with inappropriate behaviors. Punishment is not synonymous with physical abuse. A punisher is anything that decreases behavior. It can be very mild, like a frown or saying "no." We sometimes accidentally punish behavior when we are trying to reinforce it. Praise to some children is embarrasing. Consequently, they are less likely to behave in a way that will result in praise.

... ACCENTUATE THE POSITIVE ... ELIMINATE THE NEGATIVE ... AND DON'T MESS WITH MR. IN-BETWEEN

In general, punishment should not be used until several attempts have been made to use reinforcement to change a behavior. Unquestionably there are instances in which punishment, at least in the technical sense of the term, needs to be given. That is, certain behaviors need to be decreased. But most of us are quick to tune in to the bad. Try tuning in to the good. It's a little more work at first, but it is better for everyone concerned. Another procedure that can be used to avoid the use of punishment is to ignore behavior. This often results in "extinguishing" the inappropriate behavior.

— REMEMBER —

For reinforcement or punishment to be effective it should be given fairly **soon after** the behavior has occurred. It should **not** be given before the behavior occurs. If it is given before, the problem behaviors are likely to increase. The consequence must be more than a promise or idle threat. It must occur!

REVIEW

Let's review what has been said about applying consequences to behavior:

- Behavior is learned.

- Reinforcers increase behavior.

- Punishers decrease behavior.

- Be consistent.

- Different people like different things.

- There are social, activity, and tangible reinforcers.

- Use "natural" reinforcers whenever possible.

- Administer reinforcement (or punishment) **after** the behavior, **not** before.

SHAPING BEHAVIORS

An important factor to consider is how fast a child is expected to change. A child who has a behavior disorder would have great difficulty in immediately learning an entirely new behavior. He or she should be gradually shaped toward behaving differently.

SMALL STEPS TOWARD A GOAL

NEW BEHAVIOR

Shaping means successive approximations or small steps toward a goal. A behavior like being nice to others might be broken down as follows:

Schedule	Steps
1st week	Say 1 "nice thing" to someone each day.
2nd week	Say 2 "nice things" to someone each day.
3rd week	Say 2 "nice things" to someone each day plus one "good deed".
4th week	Say 2 "nice things" plus 2 "good deeds".

Because we have seen "miraculous" changes, we sometimes come to expect them. Expecting an "obnoxious" child to be immediately "helpful" and "nice" toward others is to invite failure. Starting with a small goal and gradually increasing expectations gives the child a much greater chance of success. It takes time to learn inappropriate behaviors. It will take time to unlearn them and to learn new appropriate behaviors.

MEASUREMENT AND GRAPHING

Because behavior generally changes slowly it is important to have a way of detecting that change. We must constantly be aware of the changes being made in behavior disordered children. If behaviors are measured regularly then the effectiveness of the procedures used can be evaluated more adequately.

Two measurement procedures will be discussed which are particularly suited to classroom and home settings. These are:

(1) Frequency
of occurrence
(tallying)

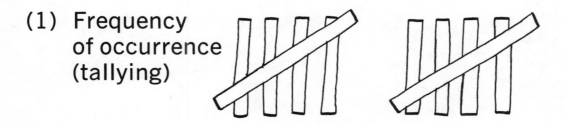

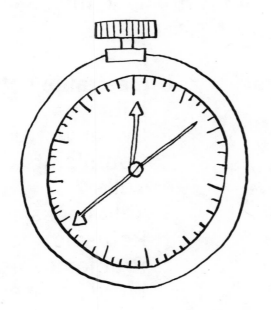

(2) Duration
of occurrence
(timing)

Change is often measured by counting behaviors. Tallying the number of times a behavior occurs is a fairly simple procedure. Each time the behavior occurs it is tallied.

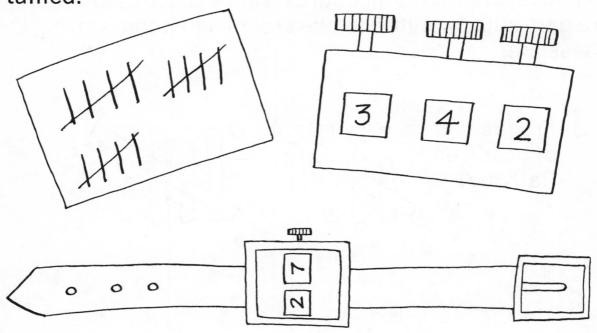

Behaviors that are easy to tally are such things as the number of:

Desirable behaviors
Compliments
Helping on jobs
 around the house:
 Making the bed
 Pick-up dishes
 Garbage out
 Pick-up room
Math problems
 completed
Pages read
Problems answered

Undesirable behaviors
Hits
Swear words
Complaints
Yells
Talk-backs
Refusals
Problems missed
Words missed

Some behaviors are measured best by timing them since they may occur for very different lengths of time. An example is being out-of-seat in class. To be out-of-seat once in a day does not tell us much. The child may have been out-of-seat for one minute or one hour.

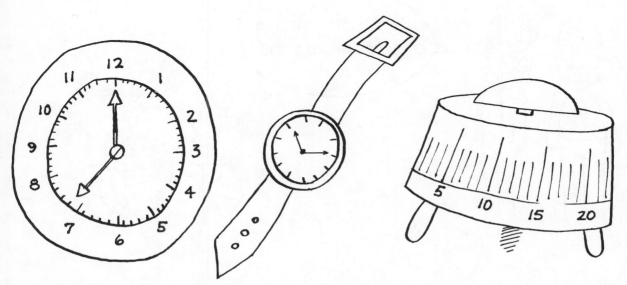

Behaviors that are measured best by timing are:

Desirable Home Behaviors
Playing with others
Working on-task
Eating (for under-eaters)

Undesirable Home Behaviors
Pouting
Crying
Screaming
Nail-biting
Eating (for over-eaters)

Desirable School Behaviors
On-task working
Talking (for shy child)

Undesirable School Behaviors
Off-task
Talking (for an outgoing child)

81

There are many behaviors that could be listed which could be tallied or timed in home or school settings. Those on the previous pages are intended to help the reader think of others. With regard to these behaviors, there are cases when what is seen as positive for one child . . .

. . . may be seen as negative for another.

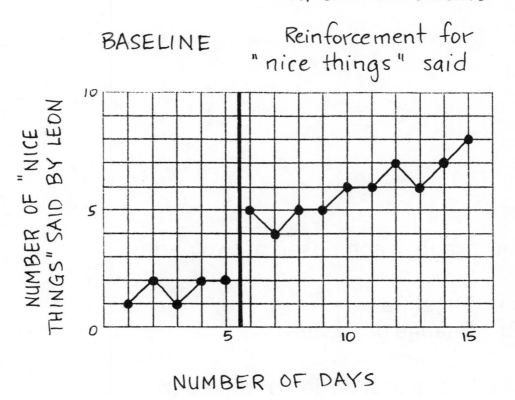

PHASE I
CHANGE PROCEDURE

BASELINE   Reinforcement for
"nice things" said

NUMBER OF DAYS

It is especially helpful if changed behavior can be recorded in a manner that is as graphic as possible. To visually represent the improvements of a behavior disordered child the parent or teacher can graph the change over time. Above is a graph of a hostile child's "nice things said" to others.

This graph is composed of two parts:

(1)   Baseline
(2)   Change procedure

Baseline is that period of time during which measurements of behavior were taken but no changes were made in how the child was treated.

Change procedure is the period of time during which a new procedure was used to help the child develop a new behavior.

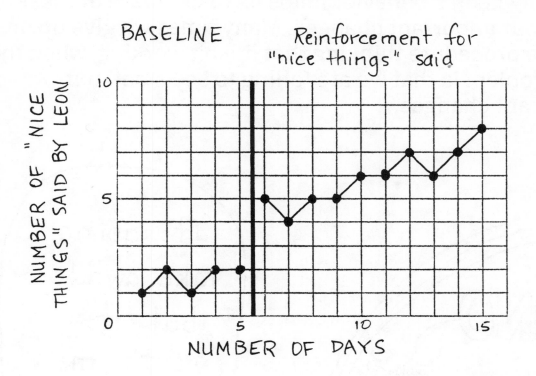

PHASE I
CHANGE PROCEDURE

BASELINE   Reinforcement for "nice things" said

Y-axis: NUMBER OF "NICE THINGS" SAID BY LEON

X-axis: NUMBER OF DAYS

This chart shows that during baseline Leon said very few "nice things" to others until he was reinforced for that kind of behavior. Each day he gets a little better at engaging in more sociable behavior. As we can see, he is making small steps toward improvement.

Charting Leon's behavior helps us to be aware of these small but important changes. Many times we give up on a change procedure thinking that it isn't working, when the real problem is that we are failing to see small but important changes.

REVIEW

The important points to remember from the section on **Shaping Behaviors** and the section on **Measurement and Graphing** are:

- Don't expect too much change too soon.

- Use successive approximations.

- Detecting changes, even small ones, on a regular basis is important.

- Frequency of occurrence (tallying) and duration of occurrence (timing) are two techniques for measuring change.

- Visual representation of measured behavior is very useful, displaying **baseline** and **change procedure** data.

APPLIED EXAMPLES IN SCHOOL AND HOME SETTINGS

The last section of this chapter will present two actual case studies. One is a school problem; the other is home related. They are intended to help teachers and parents see how behavioral principles can be applied to children with behavior disorders.

SCHOOL EXAMPLE

Loretta was a very shy girl. She hid her head in her desk whenever the teacher asked her a question in class. This was unusual behavior indeed, severe enough to qualify her, sooner or later, as behavior disordered.

Loretta's teacher decided to count the number of times she put her head in her desk when asked a question. The teacher found Loretta did this every time she was asked to respond. The teacher measured the behavior by tallying, since the length of occurrence did not vary much from one time to the next.

After obtaining several days of baseline data, Loretta's teacher decided to try to change this head-in-desk behavior. For several more days she used a reinforcer plus a "cueing procedure." That is, she would first ask other children the question that she intended to ask Loretta. She would then praise these other children.

This cueing procedure provided Loretta with the correct answer, as well as the strong possiblity of reinforcement (lavish teacher praise). This made the situation much less threatening for Loretta. She saw pleasant consequences and was provided with the correct answer. Notice the small step arranged for Loretta! The teacher started with a relatively easy step toward a goal.

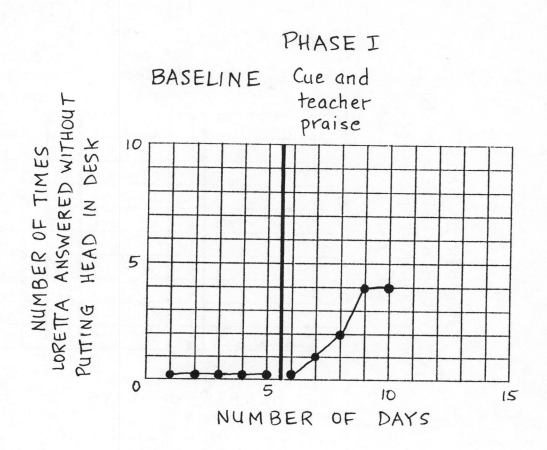

Next, the teacher asked Loretta the question. In the beginning Loretta's progress was slow. When asked a question she still tended to put her head in her desk, but not as often. That's a step toward improvement.

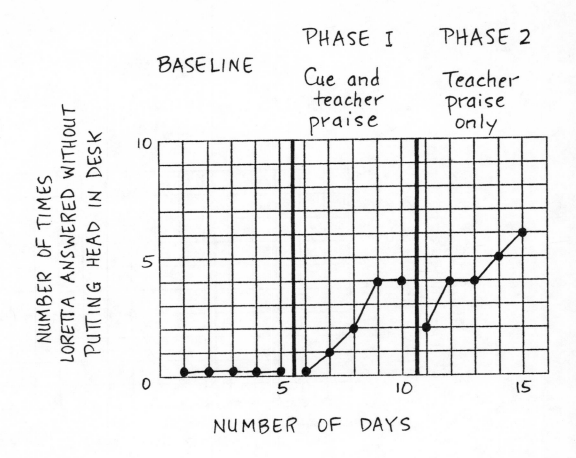

BASELINE   PHASE 1   PHASE 2

Cue and   Teacher
teacher   praise
praise   only

NUMBER OF TIMES LORETTA ANSWERED WITHOUT PUTTING HEAD IN DESK

NUMBER OF DAYS

Loretta's teacher went a step further. She continued to praise Loretta, but did not ask other children the question first. Instead she asked very simple questions which she was sure Loretta knew. Loretta continued to improve under this new condition.

Through this step by step approach, Loretta soon began to respond like other children. She did not need "artificial" circumstances. Reinforcement, shaping, consistency, and measurement paid off. Loretta was much less like a behavior disordered child.

HOME EXAMPLE

Leon was very noncommunicative, especially around adults. No one seemed to know why. He rarely talked to his teacher and never talked to neighbors. Despite prodding and admonishments from his parents, they were unable to get Leon to talk to adults.

After consulting with the school psychologist they decided to begin a home-based change program for their son. The goal was to enable Leon to freely speak with neighborhood adults.

They decided to accentuate the positive. The first step in helping Leon speak to adults was to get him to nonverbally interact with them. To achieve this, they regularly sent Leon to the neighbors to borrow things. Each neighbor was contacted ahead of time so that he or she knew what Leon would be picking up for his parents. No words were required on Leon's part.

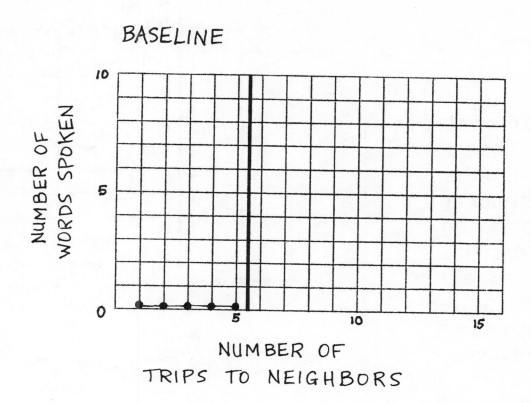

BASELINE

NUMBER OF WORDS SPOKEN

NUMBER OF
TRIPS TO NEIGHBORS

For the series of days that this was done, Leon never spoke when sent to the neighbors. This is depicted in the graph above. Baseline shows no words spoken by Leon.

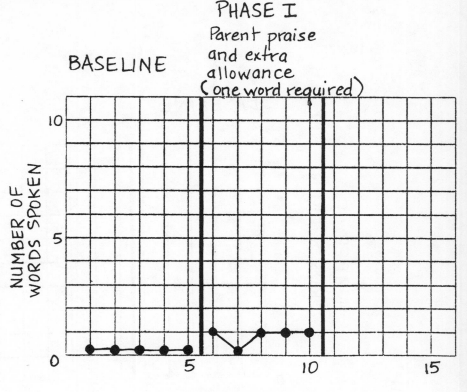

PHASE I
Parent praise
and extra
allowance
(one word required)

NUMBER OF
WORDS SPOKEN

NUMBER OF
TRIPS TO NEIGHBORS

The next step was to send Leon to the neighbors on errands for his parents. This time Leon was required to say **one** word—yes. Each time he said "yes" his parents would praise him for having "talked" with the neighbors. This talking also earned him extra allowance. The data for this phase is shown in the graph.

Do you want to use our mower?

YEP!

100

The next step was to have Leon say a very short sentence—three or more words. The neighbor usually asked, "What do you want, Leon?" Leon would have to respond "I want a _____" or some variation of that sentence. The data for this final phase are shown opposite. They indicate that his parents were achieving success with this home-based change program.

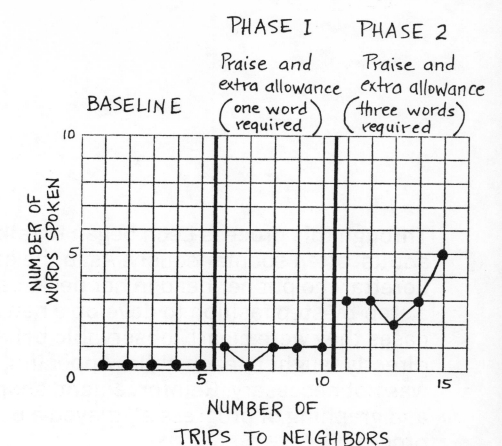

Through this process Leon began to talk more with adults, often spontaneously. As in the earlier example of Loretta who put her head in her desk, Leon was helped in a step-by-step fashion to develop a new behavior. In both cases they were clearly observable behaviors which were directly taught to each child. Appealing to inner causes was not necessary. Reinforcement, shaping, consistency, and graphing of progress all played a part in this change process.

It is hoped that teachers and parents will be more inclined to deal with behavior disorders as the results of environmental causes. Those who have adopted such an approach have found that many of the problems of children can be successfully resolved. Such an approach helps parents and teachers to see what they can do, as opposed to being forced to dismiss the problem because the cause resides in the child.

Appendix A

Appendix A includes a checklist of steps to be considered in program development. This list is designed to help you organize your approach to problems in a systematic behavioral manner. Sample data sheets are also included enabling you to graph the child's behavior. If you don't graph the behavior, how will you know if you are affecting change?

STEPS TOWARD SUCCESS WITH A BEHAVIOR DISORDERED CHILD

1. State the general problem.

2. Narrow the problem to a manageable size.
   A) Define 1, 2, or 3 small steps toward a new behavior.
   B) Select one of these on which you will begin.

3. Select a behavior measurement system.
   A) Frequency measurement
   B) Duration measurement.

4. Collect data on behavior for 5-8 days (baseline).

5. Select change procedure (Phase I).
   A) Reinforcement
   B) Punishment.

6. If necessary, move to Phase II. If results are satisfactory in Phase I you may not need to move to Phase II, unless more new skills are needed to develop appropriate behaviors.

CHILD'S NAME _____ DATE BEGAN _____ MEASUREMENT SYSTEM

GENERAL PROBLEM _____ FREQUENCY _____

DURATION _____

BASELINE | PHASE #
CHANGE PROCEDURE: | PHASE #
CHANGE PROCEDURE: | PHASE #
CHANGE PROCEDURE:

BEHAVIOR

DATE(S)

DAYS

STEPS TOWARD SUCCESS WITH A BEHAVIOR DISORDERED CHILD

1. State the general problem.

2. Narrow the problem to a manageable size.
   A) Define 1, 2, or 3 small steps toward a new behavior.
   B) Select one of these on which you will begin.

3. Select a behavior measurement system.
   A) Frequency measurement
   B) Duration measurement.

4. Collect data on behavior for 5-8 days (baseline).

5. Select change procedure (Phase I).
   A) Reinforcement
   B) Punishment.

6. If necessary, move to Phase II. If results are satisfactory in Phase I you may not need to move to Phase II, unless more new skills are needed to develop appropriate behaviors.

CHILD'S NAME —————————— DATE BEGAN —————————— MEASUREMENT SYSTEM ——————————

GENERAL PROBLEM ——————————————————————————————————— FREQUENCY ——————————

DURATION ——————————

BASELINE   PHASE #   PHASE #   PHASE #
            CHANGE PROCEDURE: CHANGE PROCEDURE: CHANGE PROCEDURE:

BEHAVIOR

DATE(S)

DAYS

107

STEPS TOWARD SUCCESS WITH A BEHAVIOR DISORDERED CHILD

1. State the general problem.

2. Narrow the problem to a manageable size.
   A) Define 1, 2, or 3 small steps toward a new behavior.
   B) Select one of these on which you will begin.

3. Select a behavior measurement system.
   A) Frequency measurement
   B) Duration measurement.

4. Collect data on behavior for 5-8 days (baseline).

5. Select change procedure (Phase I).
   A) Reinforcement
   B) Punishment.

6. If necessary, move to Phase II. If results are satisfactory in Phase I you may not need to move to Phase II, unless more new skills are needed to develop appropriate behaviors.

CHILD'S NAME _____ DATE BEGAN _____ MEASUREMENT SYSTEM _____

GENERAL PROBLEM _____   FREQUENCY _____

                                                    DURATION _____

BASELINE   PHASE # _____   PHASE # _____   PHASE # _____
            CHANGE PROCEDURE: CHANGE PROCEDURE: CHANGE PROCEDURE:

BEHAVIOR

DATE(S)   DAYS

109

STEPS TOWARD SUCCESS WITH A BEHAVIOR DISORDERED CHILD

1. State the general problem.

2. Narrow the problem to a manageable size.
   A) Define 1, 2, or 3 small steps toward a new behavior.
   B) Select one of these on which you will begin.

3. Select a behavior measurement system.
   A) Frequency measurement
   B) Duration measurement.

4. Collect data on behavior for 5-8 days (baseline).

5. Select change procedure (Phase I).
   A) Reinforcement.
   B) Punishment.

6. If necessary, move to Phase II. If results are satisfactory in Phase I you may not need to move to Phase II, unless more new skills are needed to develop appropriate behaviors.

CHILD'S NAME _____ DATE BEGAN _____ MEASUREMENT SYSTEM

GENERAL PROBLEM _____ FREQUENCY _____

DURATION _____

PHASE #
CHANGE PROCEDURE:

PHASE #
CHANGE PROCEDURE:

PHASE #
CHANGE PROCEDURE:

PHASE #
CHANGE PROCEDURE:

BASELINE

BEHAVIOR

DATE(S)

DAYS

111

STEPS TOWARD SUCCESS WITH A BEHAVIOR DISORDERED CHILD

1. State the general problem.

2. Narrow the problem to a manageable size.
   A)   Define 1, 2, or 3 small steps toward a new behavior.
   B)   Select one of these on which you will begin.

3. Select a behavior measurement system.
   A)   Frequency measurement
   B)   Duration measurement.

4. Collect data on behavior for 5-8 days (baseline).

5. Select change procedure (Phase I).
   A)   Reinforcement
   B)   Punishment.

6. If necessary, move to Phase II. If results are satisfactory in Phase I you may not need to move to Phase II, unless more new skills are needed to develop appropriate behaviors.

CHILD'S NAME _____ DATE BEGAN _____ MEASUREMENT SYSTEM

GENERAL PROBLEM _____   FREQUENCY _____

                                                          DURATION _____

BASELINE   PHASE #   PHASE #   PHASE #
                  CHANGE PROCEDURE: CHANGE PROCEDURE: CHANGE PROCEDURE:

BEHAVIOR

DATE(S)   DAYS

113

STEPS TOWARD SUCCESS WITH A BEHAVIOR DISORDERED CHILD

1. State the general problem.

2. Narrow the problem to a manageable size.
   A) Define 1, 2, or 3 small steps toward a new behavior.
   B) Select one of these on which you will begin.

3. Select a behavior measurement system.
   A) Frequency measurement
   B) Duration measurement.

4. Collect data on behavior for 5-8 days (baseline).

5. Select change procedure (Phase I).
   A) Reinforcement
   B) Punishment.

6. If necessary, move to Phase II. If results are satisfactory in Phase I you may not need to move to Phase II, unless more new skills are needed to develop appropriate behaviors.

CHILD'S NAME _____ DATE BEGAN _____ MEASUREMENT SYSTEM

GENERAL PROBLEM _____ FREQUENCY _____

DURATION _____

BASELINE | PHASE # _____ CHANGE PROCEDURE: | PHASE # _____ CHANGE PROCEDURE: | PHASE # _____ CHANGE PROCEDURE:

BEHAVIOR

DATE(S)

DAYS

115

STEPS TOWARD SUCCESS WITH A BEHAVIOR DISORDERED CHILD

1. State the general problem.

2. Narrow the problem to a manageable size
   A) Define 1, 2, or 3 small steps toward a new behavior.
   B) Select one of these on which you will begin.

3. Select a behavior measurement system.
   A) Frequency measurement
   B) Duration measurement.

4. Collect data on behavior for 5-8 days (baseline).

5. Select change procedure (Phase I).
   A) Reinforcement
   B) Punishment.

6. If necessary, move to Phase II. If results are satisfactory in Phase I you may not need to move to Phase II, unless more new skills are needed to develop appropriate behaviors.

CHILD'S NAME _____ DATE BEGAN _____ MEASUREMENT SYSTEM _____

GENERAL PROBLEM _____

FREQUENCY _____

DURATION _____

BASELINE | PHASE #
CHANGE PROCEDURE: | PHASE #
CHANGE PROCEDURE: | PHASE #
CHANGE PROCEDURE:

BEHAVIOR

DAYS

DATE(S)

117

STEPS TOWARD SUCCESS WITH A BEHAVIOR DISORDERED CHILD

1. State the general problem.

2. Narrow the problem to a manageable size.
   A) Define 1, 2, or 3 small steps toward a new behavior.
   B) Select one of these on which you will begin.

3. Select a behavior measurement system.
   A) Frequency measurement
   B) Duration measurement.

4. Collect data on behavior for 5-8 days (baseline).

5. Select change procedure (Phase I).
   A) Reinforcement.
   B) Punishment.

6. If necessary, move to Phase II. If results are satisfactory in Phase I you may not need to move to Phase II, unless more new skills are needed to develop appropriate behaviors.

About the Editor

Thomas N. Fairchild has his Ph.D. in School Psychology and is currently an Assistant Professor of Guidance and Counseling and Coordinator of the School Psychology Training Program at the University of Idaho. Dr. Fairchild earned his Bachelors, Masters, and Specialist degrees at the University of Idaho. He received his Ph.D. from the University of Iowa in 1974. The editor has published over a dozen journal articles in the areas of school psychology and counseling. Dr. Fairchild has worked as a teacher, counselor, and school psychologist. He has had the privilege of working with students across all grade levels, and in his opinion they are all special.

About the Author

A. Lee Parks is an Associate Professor of Special Education at the University of Idaho. He began his professional career as a school psychologist in the State of Washington. He attended the University of Kansas where he received his Ph.D. During this time he worked as a Research Trainee for the Bureau of Child Research. After receiving his doctorate he accepted a position at The Ohio State University where he held a joint appointment with the Nisonger Center for Mental Retardation and the Faculty for Exceptional Children. He is presently at the University of Idaho.

About the Illustrator

Everyone can draw—some with more competence then others. Occasionally you find someone who is exceptionally gifted in a particular facet of drawing. Danial B. Fairchild is that someone. He is a highly talented cartoonist with a style that is uniquely his own. His achievements include cartoons printed in newspapers and magazines, and most recently two paperbacks entitled **Cowtoons** (Artcraft Press, Nampa, Idaho), which depict, in a very humorous way the life of cowboys.